Little Dreamers Acrostics

Poetry Explorers

Edited By Byron Tobolik

First published in Great Britain in 2025 by:

Young Writers
Remus House
Coltsfoot Drive
Peterborough
PE2 9BF
Telephone: 01733 890066
Website: www.youngwriters.co.uk

All Rights Reserved
Book Design by Ashley Janson
© Copyright Contributors 2024
Softback ISBN 978-1-83685-069-4
Printed and bound in the UK by BookPrintingUK
Website: www.bookprintinguk.com
YB0621A

Foreword

Welcome Reader,

For Young Writers' latest competition Little Dreamers, we asked primary school pupils to write an acrostic poem. They could write about an animal, their favourite person, themselves or something from their imagination – anything at all! The acrostic is a fantastic introduction to poetry writing as it comes with a built-in structure, allowing children to focus on their creativity and vocabulary choice.

We live and breathe creativity here at Young Writers and we want to pass our love of the written word onto the next generation – what better way to do that than to celebrate their writing by publishing it in a book!

Featuring poems on a range of topics, this anthology is brimming with imagination and creativity, showcasing the blossoming writing skills of these young poets. They have brought their ideas to life using the power of words, resulting in some brilliant and fun acrostic poems!

Each awesome poet in this book should be super proud of themselves! We hope you will delight in these poems as much as we have.

Contents

Barrow Island Community Primary School, Barrow-In-Furness

Isaiah Marshall (6)	1
Azlan Ijaz (6)	2
Lochlan Dugdale (6)	3
Jocelyn Atkinson (6)	4
Teddy Bushby (6)	5
Charley Humphrey (6)	6
Jake Wilson (7)	7
Joy Fayemi (7)	8
Emie Harris (6)	9
Olivia Askey (6)	10
Lucas Shannon (6)	11
Anamika Athiyottil (6)	12
Jadie Curtis (6) & Amber-May Jefferson (6)	13
Freddie Hayman (6)	14
Azeezah Shoyombo (7)	15

Brockworth Primary Academy, Brockworth

Lola-Lee Deacon (6)	16
Ivy Sanderson (6)	17
Liliana Reeves (6)	18
Milan Love (6)	19
Harper Sweet (6)	20
Chayse Greenway (6)	21
Abigail Hicking (6)	22
Marius Bowkett (6)	23
Ethan Jibu (6)	24
Thea-Rose Marsh (6)	25
Eloise Tindall-Herbert (6)	26
Ati Sumaina (6)	27

Florence Langley (6)	28
River Gilmore (6)	29

Chase Side Primary School, Enfield

Ayoub Lahdiri (6)	30
Bellatrix Kandasamy (7)	31
Kathryn Austin (6)	32
Ellis Moseley-Cove (7)	33
Yuvaan Thakur (6)	34
Ludovica Cannas (7)	35
Joseph Alidu (6)	36
Shazfa Khan (6)	37
Serayah Walker-Henry (6)	38
Ayman Omar (6)	39
Daniel Ramage (6)	40
Hanusree Balaji (6)	41
Lola-Belle Evensen (7)	42
Mia Kushi (6)	43
Frederick Lyte (6)	44
Alexantro Tsepele (7)	45
Archie Furrer (6)	46
Sinethi Ariyasinghage (6)	47
Lorel Maci (6)	48
Jack Basquil (6)	49
Davia Simbo (6)	50
Rico Townsend (6)	51
Anthony Alidu (6)	52
Muhammad Wahaj (7)	53
Firefunmi Paul-Festus (6)	54
Reggie Whitaker (6)	55
Ceren Emin (6)	56
Kyle Savill (6)	57

Edge Grove School, Aldenham Village

Chloe Roper (6)	58
Theo Ahdan (6)	59
Zakaria Datoo (6)	60
Jagger Fox Conway (6)	61
Jay Patel (6)	62
Arlo Devrimoz (6)	63
Ayden Chowk (6)	64
Isaac Jeraj (6)	65
Freddie Sharman (7)	66
Sophia Pavel (6)	67
Ruairi Walsham (6)	68
Ishan Lakhani (6)	69
Isabella Wilkinson (6)	70
Rishi John (6)	71
Laith-Mahdi Haji (6)	72
Cillian Witte (6)	73
Luna Rayner (6)	74
Oscar Islin (6)	75
Danyal Alikhan (6)	76
Fritz Mayo (6)	77
Tomasz Lynch (6)	78
Asher Samuel (6)	79
Aalia Mohsin (6)	80
Ayaan Shamar (6)	81
Aryan Soneji (7)	82
Nathaniel Shtrosberg (6)	83
Zakariya Charles Treadwell (6)	84
Orlaith Neill (6)	85
Isabella Stein (6)	86
Milo Hodges (6)	87
Gabriella Hilton (6)	88
Noah Rahman (6)	89
Luca Martins (6)	90
Aryan Pandya (6)	91
Leah Rosen (6)	92
Narjes Kaboul (6)	93
Jessica Scutelnicu (6)	94
Nyla Ogunsanwo (6)	95
Anaisha Saxena (6)	96

Edgeborough School, Farnham

Max Evans (6)	97
Demilade Ajelabi (6)	98
Felicity Chalkley (6)	99
Tilly Vincent (6)	100
Hugo Steele (6)	101
Max Kimberley-Bowen (6)	102
Reyan Patel (7)	103
Hugo Peachey (6)	104
Lachlan Mackenzie (6)	105
Jeremy Kelly (6)	106
Percy Sadler (6)	107
Hamish Hudson (6)	108
Emmie Gottschalk (6)	109
Liam Siegele (7)	110
Hugo Dewé-Roux (6)	111
Rita Carlile (6)	112
Laurence Fisher (7)	113

Hebburn Lakes Primary School, Hebburn

Lyla-Mae Reynolds (6)	114
Miller McGonnell (6)	115
Alisha Marshall (6)	116
Hannah Davison (6)	117
Luke Craig (6)	118
Jessica Casey (6)	119
Millie-Rae Halliday (6)	120
Faye Whitehead (6)	121
Sophie Crumbie (6)	122
Erica Robertson (6)	123
Kendall Smurthwaite (6)	124
Phoebe Lumley (6)	125
Kade Loughran (6)	126

Kirn Primary School, Kirn

Sienna Connelly (7)	127
Ella Dickson (6)	128
Rory Gray (7)	129
Jay Mackay (6)	130
Dylan Stevenson (7)	131

Suri McGinnigal (6)	132
Alyvia Larkins (7)	133
Bjorn Collier (6)	134
Mason MacLean (6)	135
Sara Brivkalns (6)	136
Ella Campbell (6)	137
Emily Kennedy (7)	138
Fergus Allison (7)	139
Andrew Gorman (6)	140
Arlo Poynter-Dalton (7)	141

Portsmouth High School, Southsea

Felicia Wang (6)	142
Peony Marsh (5)	143
Sofia Kadinopoulos (5)	144
Addison Knight (6)	145
Payton Law (6)	146
Lula Peck (5)	147
Blossom Morgan (5)	148
Alazne Currie (5)	149
Olivia Cullen-Taylor (6)	150
Mateya Asenov (5)	151
Betty Woolridge (6)	152
Ava Norris (5)	153
Neve Worrall (5)	154
Abbiah Gunton (7)	155
Ruona Osigho (6)	156
Hallie Lewis-Gregory (7)	157
Layla Belcher (6)	158
Raphaella Tozzi (7)	159
Alba Shireby (6)	160

St Joseph's Catholic Primary School, Uttoxeter

Edward Crawford (6)	161
Oliver Rathbone (6)	162
Arthur McNicol (6)	163
Bodhi Raby (6)	164
Katya Pastushenko (8)	165
Arla Fearnett (6)	166
Freddie Sutton (6)	167

Ginny Rushton (6)	168
Evie Gill (6)	169
Ella Peach (6)	170
Jozef Korista-Redfern (6)	171
Louis Matthew Young (6)	172
Ashleigh Roberts (6)	173
Cora McCutcheon (6)	174
Phoebe Grattage (6)	175
Iona O'Neill (6)	176
Irina Babacea (6)	177
Beau Bromage (6)	178
Freddie H (6)	179
Freya Jeziorska (6)	180
Perrie Stephens (6)	181
Shayne Felix Fernandes (6)	182

St Patrick's RC Primary School, Consett

Hannah Bushby (6)	183
Evie Henderson (7)	184
Harry Richardson (6)	185
Lydia Murphy (6)	186
James Ellison (6)	187
Amelia Tennant (6)	188
Daisy Cooke (6)	189
Kaylam-James Walton (7)	190
Rhys Hughes (6)	191
Ivy Dorritt (6)	192
Jamie Dixon (6)	193
Theo Spencer (6)	194
Tia-Louise Hester (6)	195
Aria Joyce (6)	196
Noah Edward (6)	197
Oliver O'Keefe (7)	198
Joseph Richardson (6)	199
George Wilson (6)	200
Isla-Grace Robinson (6)	201
Lydia O'Rourke (6)	202
Ella MacGregor (7)	203

Staines Preparatory School, Knowle Green

Odysseas Papamichos Chronakis (6)	204
Rohan Sharma (6)	205
Maitreyi Patil (6)	206
Zoie Pitroda (6)	207
Bella Patel (6)	208
Nirbhay Singh (6)	209
Leya Kareer Gupta (6)	210
Arjan Gill (6)	211
Tawanda Tapiwa (6)	212

The Poems

Chocolatier

C hocolate is delicious
H ot chocolate is so creamy
O h so tasty!
C hocolate is velvety
O h so smooth
L ick your lips
A re you coming to the factory?
T o the chocolate river, we go
I fell into the soft cotton candy
E xtremely magical
R are chocolate.

Isaiah Marshall (6)
Barrow Island Community Primary School, Barrow-In-Furness

Dentist

D entists take out teeth.
E ating sweets will make your teeth break.
N urses check your teeth too many times.
T eeth will fail you if you eat too much chocolate
I will take your teeth out, so stay still.
S o remember to brush your teeth.
T eeth become dentures when you are old.

Azlan Ijaz (6)
Barrow Island Community Primary School, Barrow-In-Furness

Invisible

I nvincible
N o way to find me
V isit the bad guys
I ncredible
S uperpowers
I n my room, I can disappear
B e the best
L et's rob a bank
E vil.

Lochlan Dugdale (6)
Barrow Island Community Primary School, Barrow-In-Furness

Mrs Wonka

M agical
R are
S urprise

W onka Bars
O h, what delicious treats
N ever doubt yourself
K eep out of the chocolate river
A mazing.

Jocelyn Atkinson (6)
Barrow Island Community Primary School, Barrow-In-Furness

Strength

S trong
T ear apart cars
R ace bad guys
E nergy
N o, don't eat the car!
G et away
T ease the bad guys
H ide.

Teddy Bushby (6)
Barrow Island Community Primary School, Barrow-In-Furness

Insects

I 'm scared!
N asty pests
S uper cute butterflies
E xtremely terrifying
C lose the windows
T oo scary
S quish them.

Charley Humphrey (6)
Barrow Island Community Primary School, Barrow-In-Furness

Beetles

B eetles for breakfast
E vil
E at the bugs
T errifying
L ittle, creepy legs
E xtremely dangerous
S limy and stinky.

Jake Wilson (7)
Barrow Island Community Primary School, Barrow-In-Furness

Nigeria

N ight lights are so bright
I ncredible
G reat
E xcellent
R eally scorching
I nside to keep cool
A mazing tricks.

Joy Fayemi (7)
Barrow Island Community Primary School, Barrow-In-Furness

Clowns

C ircus
L aughing and giggling
O h! Hello, kids!
W e are going to the circus
N ose
S queezy red nose.

Emie Harris (6)
Barrow Island Community Primary School, Barrow-In-Furness

Spiders

S urprise!
P et
I nside your house
D angerous
E ats dead flies
R eally terrifying
S cary!

Olivia Askey (6)
Barrow Island Community Primary School, Barrow-In-Furness

Strong

S trength
T ear apart cars
R ip apart buildings
O h, don't do that
N ever give up
G o for it!

Lucas Shannon (6)
Barrow Island Community Primary School, Barrow-In-Furness

Teacher

T each fun lessons
E xciting
A mazing
C all me Miss
H elp children
E xcellent
R ight.

Anamika Athiyottil (6)
Barrow Island Community Primary School, Barrow-In-Furness

Spiders

S urprise!
P et
I nside your house
D angerous
E ats flies
R eally terrifying
S cary!

Jadie Curtis (6) & Amber-May Jefferson (6)
Barrow Island Community Primary School, Barrow-In-Furness

Flying

F loating in the sky
L et me go!
Y es, I can fly
I nvincible
N ever give up
G o up to space.

Freddie Hayman (6)
Barrow Island Community Primary School, Barrow-In-Furness

America

A mazing
M agical
E xciting
R ides
I ncredible
C olossal
A mazing and beautiful.

Azeezah Shoyombo (7)
Barrow Island Community Primary School, Barrow-In-Furness

Protect Animals

P arrots have colourful wings
R ed pandas like bamboo
O ctopuses squirt ink
T ortoises move slowly
E very animal is special
C aring for animals is a job
T he tallest land animal is a giraffe

A nimals are cute
N ever make an animal sad
I n the world, animals are good
M ight bite you
A nimals are brilliant friends
L ions are big cats
S o protect them!

Lola-Lee Deacon (6)
Brockworth Primary Academy, Brockworth

Contortionist

C an you do a backbend
O r can you do the splits?
N ever give up trying
T o do a wall split
O r you can do a
R ight leg scale
T he right thing to do
I s a leap
O h, this is fun
N ow, look!
I sn't this cool?
S ee that you are shining
T oday is fun.

Ivy Sanderson (6)
Brockworth Primary Academy, Brockworth

Gymnastics

G ymnastics is good
Y es, it's especially great
M y favourite is practising
N o skills
A mazing splits
S kills are the best
T errific swinging and rolling
I t is good on the balance beam
C ool kicking is the best
S uch energetic routines.

Liliana Reeves (6)
Brockworth Primary Academy, Brockworth

Zookeeper

  Z ookeepers help animals
  O ranges help animals get better
  O ranges are really good for animals
  K oalas are so cute
  E lephants are so big
  E lephants' ears are so big
  P andas are black and white
  E lephants are lovely
  R hinos are so big.

Milan Love (6)
Brockworth Primary Academy, Brockworth

Ballerina

B allerinas are beautiful
A ll of them do a good job
L eaping everywhere
L ovely dresses
E chappé
R eally good twirls
I love ballet
N ice moves
A big leap.

Harper Sweet (6)
Brockworth Primary Academy, Brockworth

Swimmer

S wimming is good
W inning is the best thing in swimming
I t is the best for me
M y mum loves swimming
M aybe I'll be in the Olympics
E xcited for swimming
R eally love swimming.

Chayse Greenway (6)
Brockworth Primary Academy, Brockworth

Flamingo

F abulous animals
L oyal animals
A s pink as a rose
M agical, mystical birds
I love flamingos
N aughty beaks
G raceful fliers
O r they could be white.

Abigail Hicking (6)
Brockworth Primary Academy, Brockworth

Police

P olice arrest bad people
O fficer
L ike to be a police officer
I like being a police officer
C ar is a police car
E thical police officer.

Marius Bowkett (6)
Brockworth Primary Academy, Brockworth

Artist

A rt is good
R ating of art is very good
T o me, art is the best
I like art
S everal types of art are good
T he art can be dark or light.

Ethan Jibu (6)
Brockworth Primary Academy, Brockworth

Teacher

T he kids are amazing
E njoy work
A lways smiling
C reating fun lessons
H ard work
E asy work for one day
R eading is so good.

Thea-Rose Marsh (6)
Brockworth Primary Academy, Brockworth

Astronaut

A stronauts
S cience
T oday
R ussian
O n a mission
N ASA
A stronauts
U p in space
T oday.

Eloise Tindall-Herbert (6)
Brockworth Primary Academy, Brockworth

Pilot

P ilots fly jets
I like travelling
L oud noise on take-off
O n landing, I feel relaxed
T ravelling in the air is awesome.

Ati Sumaina (6)
Brockworth Primary Academy, Brockworth

Artist

A rt exhibition
R ed paint
T exture
I nk
S ketch
T alent.

Florence Langley (6)
Brockworth Primary Academy, Brockworth

Vet

V ery caring
E ven cure lobsters
T ake care of the animals.

River Gilmore (6)
Brockworth Primary Academy, Brockworth

Footballer

F ootball
O pportunity
O pportunity for Ronaldo and Haaland
T he Champions League is the best
B ecause Real Madrid are the best
A pes can't play football
L ike humans can
L ike a cheetah, I can score a goal in one minute
E veryone should play football against Liverpool
R onaldo is the best player in the world.

Ayoub Lahdiri (6)
Chase Side Primary School, Enfield

Rainbow

R ainbows are very colourful and sparkly
A nd I love how they shine so brightly in the blue sky
I spot them in the sky and say, "Wow, a beautiful rainbow!"
N early everybody loves rainbows and I do too
B ees make sweet honey that tastes like a rainbow
O h yay, the rainbow came out
W oah! The rainbow is so bright.

Bellatrix Kandasamy (7)
Chase Side Primary School, Enfield

Unicorn

U nicorns are nice
N ice and beautiful for a unicorn
I love unicorns so much and I bet you do too
C olourful and the unicorn lives on a rainbow in the sky
O h, they can fly and they can also live on the ground
R eally, I would like to play
N o, don't leave me. You are nice and beautiful. I love you, Unicorn.

Kathryn Austin (6)
Chase Side Primary School, Enfield

Football

F ootball is my favourite sport
O utside it's good because the other team can score too
O ffside means it's the goalie's ball
T ry to flick it up
B all spins in the air when we flick it up
A ll footballs are good in 2024
L ove to kick it around the pitch
L ove to slide-tackle people.

Ellis Moseley-Cove (7)
Chase Side Primary School, Enfield

Football

F ootball is a good sport
O ther footballers are like goalies
O n the field, teams compete
T he football players are fast
B alls are hard and patchy
A football stadium is very big
L osing means you lost a match
L ights out in a dark stadium means the match is over.

Yuvaan Thakur (6)
Chase Side Primary School, Enfield

Soft Plays

S oft plays are fun
O r you could go somewhere else
F ind a special place
T here are slides and monkey bars

P lay all day long
L ove to play and climb
A nd you can do awesome jumps
Y ou can do anything
S o go to a soft play!

Ludovica Cannas (7)
Chase Side Primary School, Enfield

Soft Play

S oft plays are fun
O n the top of the soft play
F un and games
T ouch the pattern and you win!

P lay on the trampoline
L et go of our worries
A prize to be won
Y our games are typically fun.

Joseph Alidu (6)
Chase Side Primary School, Enfield

Unicorn

U nicorns are magical
N othing is cuter than them
I love unicorns in their den
C orn is sweet and so are they
O h my gosh, I wish I could play
R ainbows are great
N owhere to be seen, except in my dreams.

Shazfa Khan (6)
Chase Side Primary School, Enfield

Unicorn

U nicorns always fly so high
N aughty people don't see us
I like rainbows
C an we have fun every day?
O ctopuses are our friends
R ain is my favourite weather
N o one is magic like us.

Serayah Walker-Henry (6)
Chase Side Primary School, Enfield

Policeman

P lays all the time
O ften always here
L ooking everywhere
I ncredible stuff
C hasing bad guys
E xciting
M y favourite
A mazing arts
N ice and epic.

Ayman Omar (6)
Chase Side Primary School, Enfield

Diamond

D iamonds are in caves
I ncredible diamonds
A nd so many diamonds
M ore diamonds than gold
O ften in the caves
N o diamonds in schools
D azzling like the stars.

Daniel Ramage (6)
Chase Side Primary School, Enfield

Unicorn

U nicorns are sparkly
N ew unicorns are the best
I am the best unicorn
C ute little unicorn
O h, I am so pretty
R oni is the unicorn's name
N ice unicorn.

Hanusree Balaji (6)
Chase Side Primary School, Enfield

Unicorn

U nicorns are shiny
N ice and caring
I saw unicorns flying
C lever unicorns
O n a unicorn
R eally magical
N eed to eat rainbows.

Lola-Belle Evensen (7)
Chase Side Primary School, Enfield

Rainbow

R ainbows are nice
A mazing rainbow
I t is amazing
N ice rainbows
B rilliant colours
O range, red and blue
W onderful and bright.

Mia Kushi (6)
Chase Side Primary School, Enfield

Police

P olice are cool
O ften, they're fast
L ucky, they got doughnuts
I t is cool and fast; too fast
C ars drive really fast
E xtremely fast.

Frederick Lyte (6)
Chase Side Primary School, Enfield

Supercar

S oft seats
U mbrella top
P ink colour car
E pic car
R eally fast car
C onvertible
A mazing rides
R eally fun.

Alexantro Tsepele (7)
Chase Side Primary School, Enfield

Football

F ootball
O ffside
O ff - red card!
T ottenham
B all
A rchie Gray
L ewandowski
L ionel Messi.

Archie Furrer (6)
Chase Side Primary School, Enfield

Unicorn

U nicorns are special
N ice
I ncredible
C lever creatures
O ften flying
R ainbow sparkles
N ever bad.

Sinethi Ariyasinghage (6)
Chase Side Primary School, Enfield

Stars

S tars are so fluffy
T he stars are up in the sky
A shooting star in the sky
R eally amazing stars
S tars are amazing.

Lorel Maci (6)
Chase Side Primary School, Enfield

Football

F ootball
O ffside
O ut
T ottenham
B olton
A rsenal
L ong throw
L eroy Sané.

Jack Basquil (6)
Chase Side Primary School, Enfield

Unicorn

U nicorn
N ice
I like unicorns
C aring
O range unicorns
R eally fun
N eeds rainbow food.

Davia Simbo (6)
Chase Side Primary School, Enfield

Cats

C ute, playful and huggable
A nimals, I like them
T he black cat is mine
S o he is a boy and he likes cat food.

Rico Townsend (6)
Chase Side Primary School, Enfield

Dragon

D aring
R ed and black wings
A mazing monster
G reen scaly skin
O range fire
N aughty.

Anthony Alidu (6)
Chase Side Primary School, Enfield

Dragons

D ark green
R *oar!*
A mazing
G reen and
O range
N ice
S uper.

Muhammad Wahaj (7)
Chase Side Primary School, Enfield

Police

P olice
O ften help
L ives
I n need of
C are
E veryone is friendly.

Firefunmi Paul-Festus (6)
Chase Side Primary School, Enfield

Dogs

D ogs are cute
O range and brown
G etting lots of treats
S cary when they bark.

Reggie Whitaker (6)
Chase Side Primary School, Enfield

Beach

B each
E xciting
A hammock swinging
C old water
H oliday house.

Ceren Emin (6)
Chase Side Primary School, Enfield

Cars

C ars are really fast
A nd shiny
R acing really fast
S o shiny.

Kyle Savill (6)
Chase Side Primary School, Enfield

Play With Aria

P laying with Aria is so much fun
L et's laugh and giggle until the day is done
A fter school, we'll go to Smiggle to shop
Y es, let's buy bunnies that hop!

W e'll do some gymnastics until it's dark
I n the park where the dogs bark
T ogether, we'll learn some science too
H ow things work and what they do!

A ria, you're my best friend, you see!
R eally adventurous, we will always be
I n the sunshine where we can run free
A ria, remember, fun is the key!

Chloe Roper (6)
Edge Grove School, Aldenham Village

Paleontology

P terosaurs ruled the skies
A ll dinosaurs are extinct
L ived 65 million years ago
E veryone knows about dinosaurs
O ver 700 species discovered
N ew dinosaurs get discovered all the time
T -rex is the king of the dinosaurs
O nce dinosaurs ruled the Earth
L ong tails gave them balance
O viraptors were thought to steal eggs
G igantosaurus was bigger than a T-rex
Y ou can see fossils in a museum.

Theo Ahdan (6)
Edge Grove School, Aldenham Village

Footballer

F ootball is the best sport
O nly men play it, I thought
O ne day, I watched Man United
T he players were all splendid
B eating Chelsea 2-1
A t Old Trafford, under the sun
L ovely ladies in Manchester red
L eft me thinking I had been misled
E veryone is welcome to play
R ight now, come what may!

Zakaria Datoo (6)
Edge Grove School, Aldenham Village

Strength

S uperpowers strong and bright
T o face the world with all your might
R esilient heart, a lion's roar
E very challenge, you will achieve more
N ever let your energy hide
G row so strong with lots of pride
T rue strength is inside you, set it free
H eroes aren't just what you see on TV.

Jagger Fox Conway (6)
Edge Grove School, Aldenham Village

Real Madrid

R eal Madrid are the champions
E very day, playing for them
A mazing experience
L iving legends

M agical matches
A ll of the players are superstars
D ribbling across the pitch
R esults make the difference
I magine the life
D ream and believe.

Jay Patel (6)
Edge Grove School, Aldenham Village

Football

F un with my friends
O n Friday morning
O n the grass pitch
T alking and running after the
B all to score goals
A t the end, we are all celebrating
L aughing and chatting about the game
L ining up now because break is over.

Arlo Devrimoz (6)
Edge Grove School, Aldenham Village

Goalkeeper

G oalkeepers wear gloves
O nana is a great goalie
A ccuracy is key
L ove the job
K ick the ball
E ffort is important
E veryone plays as a team
P ractice makes perfect
E verything is teamwork
R esults.

Ayden Chowk (6)
Edge Grove School, Aldenham Village

Football

F un all day and night
O uch! Yellow card!
O ur ball, it is off the pitch
T *ick, tick* goes the clock
B all shoots past two players
A player scores a goal
L ots of players are hurt
L ast minute, our team scores.

Isaac Jeraj (6)
Edge Grove School, Aldenham Village

Football

F ootball is fun
O ver the crossbar and into the crowd
"O oooh!" shout the fans
T ackle, tackle, get the ball
B oot the ball into the goal
A ttack the ball and score a goal
L ong-range shot
L ob the goalie.

Freddie Sharman (7)
Edge Grove School, Aldenham Village

Winter

W inter is cold and beautiful
I cicles glisten in the sunlight
N earby, you can hear children laughing on their sledges
T he trees are covered in sparkling white snow
E verybody loves Christmas
R eally pretty decorated Christmas trees.

Sophia Pavel (6)
Edge Grove School, Aldenham Village

Footballer

F un
O n the pitch
O ne goalie on a team
T ry to score a goal
B all in the air
A lways have a captain
L ead the team
L isten to the captain
E leven players on a team
R un with the ball.

Ruairi Walsham (6)
Edge Grove School, Aldenham Village

Leopard

L eaping through the acacia trees
E lusive and camouflaged
O ne eye is always on the lookout
P ouncing on a baby impala
A thrilling sight
R ips deep into the impala's skin
D aring leopard wins again!

Ishan Lakhani (6)
Edge Grove School, Aldenham Village

Zookeeper

Z ebras are stripy
O utside is where I work
O ur zoo is brilliant
K eep the animals safe
E lephants are big
E xcited
P lease be kind to the animals
E very day is fun
R oar!

Isabella Wilkinson (6)
Edge Grove School, Aldenham Village

Duckling

D ucks like to swim
U nder the water, they dip
C ute and wet
K icking the water when they swim
L ove them so much
I t is my dream to have one
N aughty but funny
G olden like the sun.

Rishi John (6)
Edge Grove School, Aldenham Village

Safari

S tripy zebras galloping fast
A frican elephants stomping hard
F erocious lions roaring loudly
A towering giraffe chomping on trees
R hinos bashing through the leaves
I 'm so excited to be here.

Laith-Mahdi Haji (6)
Edge Grove School, Aldenham Village

Dinosaur

D angerous for cavemen
I n times long ago
N othing will stop them!
O r maybe it will...
S trange events; a volcano or meteor
A nd their
U seless tiny hands
R *oar!*

Cillian Witte (6)
Edge Grove School, Aldenham Village

Scientist

S cientists study snakes
C lever children can be scientists
I t's very interesting
E xciting
N ew ideas
T ests
I magination
S pecial
T ry new inventions.

Luna Rayner (6)
Edge Grove School, Aldenham Village

Crystal

   C rystals are magical
   R uby, opal, emerald and moonstone
   Y ou need to touch it
   S mooth is their texture
   T hey are colourful
   A ll full of energy
   L ong-lasting natural objects.

Oscar Islin (6)
Edge Grove School, Aldenham Village

Monsters

M onsters are terrifying
O h my goodness!
N ear my bedside
S taring at me
T rying to
E at me!
"R oar!" I shouted
S ending them back to their world.

Danyal Alikhan (6)
Edge Grove School, Aldenham Village

Animals

A n African fish eagle
N ighthawk hunting
I ndian taipan sunbathing
M agpies hunting small mice
A lligator resting
L eopard lying down
S nakes catching their prey.

Fritz Mayo (6)
Edge Grove School, Aldenham Village

Horses

H orses are gentle
O nly some days, they are annoying
R eally in my dreams, they are colourful
S ome are faded lavender
E verybody loves horses
S o why not have a horse?

Tomasz Lynch (6)
Edge Grove School, Aldenham Village

RAF Pilot

R escue
A eroplane
F lying Fortress

P lanes in the sky
I am brave
L ightning speed
O n the way
T yphoons are in Germany and England.

Asher Samuel (6)
Edge Grove School, Aldenham Village

Doctor

D ental kits are used for
O perations by dentists
C heck your teeth
T wice a day, brush your teeth
O r else your teeth will turn black
R ot, rot, rot!

Aalia Mohsin (6)
Edge Grove School, Aldenham Village

Kenya

K ind hearts all around
E lephants roaming in the wild
N ature so green and plentiful
Y ellow sunsets and beautiful skies
A frican drums beating all around.

Ayaan Shamar (6)
Edge Grove School, Aldenham Village

Police

P olice protect people
O ur cars, you can hear them
L ights are flashing red and blue
I can see them coming
C ars racing past
E mergency - 999.

Aryan Soneji (7)
Edge Grove School, Aldenham Village

Football

F ootball is the best
O n my team
O wn goal
T he World Cup
B ig strike
A penalty
L ove Aston Villa
L ots of players.

Nathaniel Shtrosberg (6)
Edge Grove School, Aldenham Village

Sharks

S harks are scary but baby sharks are cute
H ave sharp teeth
A re in deep waters
R eady to bite you
K ill their prey
S wim away fast!

Zakariya Charles Treadwell (6)
Edge Grove School, Aldenham Village

Puppy

P uppy, I love you
U nder the Christmas tree, there you were
P leased to see me after school
P lease puppy, come to me
Y ou are the best puppy.

Orlaith Neill (6)
Edge Grove School, Aldenham Village

Happy

H elpfulness means being kind
A nd good sportsmanship
P laydates make me happy
P resents and parties are joyful
Y ellow is a happy colour.

Isabella Stein (6)
Edge Grove School, Aldenham Village

Marley

M y cat
A lways relaxed
R eally cute
L oves to scratch our couch
E xtra soft and fluffy
Y ikes! He's caught a mouse!

Milo Hodges (6)
Edge Grove School, Aldenham Village

Pony

P onies are small and full of fun
O ut in the fields, they love to run
N eighing and playing all day long
Y ou can hear their happy songs.

Gabriella Hilton (6)
Edge Grove School, Aldenham Village

Speed

S upersonic running
P eople can't see me
E veryone sees a flash
E xhilaration is what I feel
D reaming of my adventure.

Noah Rahman (6)
Edge Grove School, Aldenham Village

Fly Up

F ly to Africa
L and and get a hotel
Y ou could fly to Madagascar

U nder the palm trees
P ast a ring-tailed lemur.

Luca Martins (6)
Edge Grove School, Aldenham Village

Sharks

S cary, sharp teeth
H ungry hunters
A ngry faces
R acing fast
K iller animals
S wim in the deep blue sea.

Aryan Pandya (6)
Edge Grove School, Aldenham Village

Artist

A rt is beautiful
R eally creative
T otally awesome
I want to be an artist
S omeday
T oday is the day.

Leah Rosen (6)
Edge Grove School, Aldenham Village

Energy

E xpert at dancing
N arjes is good at dancing
E nergy
R unning
G o to the stage
Y ou can do this.

Narjes Kaboul (6)
Edge Grove School, Aldenham Village

Doctor

D edicated to their patients
O ptimist
C aring
T houghtful
O bservant
R esponsible.

Jessica Scutelnicu (6)
Edge Grove School, Aldenham Village

Singer

S tage
I am good
N otes
G et the mic
E veryone's there
R eady.

Nyla Ogunsanwo (6)
Edge Grove School, Aldenham Village

Fairy

F riendly
A nd loving
I ntelligent
R osy cheeks
Y oung.

Anaisha Saxena (6)
Edge Grove School, Aldenham Village

Footballer

F ootball celebration
O ffside!
O ff the pitch
T he ref blows his whistle
B ooting the ball at the tall goalkeeper
A ball comes to a footballer - he shoots!
L oud cheers are coming from the big, enormous crowd
L oud cheers are coming from the footballers because they're celebrating loudly
E leven players on both sides
R ef blows his whistle because it's a red card!

Max Evans (6)
Edgeborough School, Farnham

Footballer

F ootballers are fast
O n Earth, football is a popular sport
O n Earth, the fastest player is Mbappé
T he best team is Liverpool
B eautiful trophy is the World Cup
A ll football players are strong
L ightning fast
L ove to go faster
E normous player like Palmer
R un, footballers!

Demilade Ajelabi (6)
Edgeborough School, Farnham

Snow Leopard

S uch cute creatures
N ow on our Earth
O ur job is to protect them
W hile they are endangered

L ovely creatures
E legant and cuddly
O n the rocks
P owerful teeth and claws
A nd they pounce
R unning through the mountains
D angerous animals.

Felicity Chalkley (6)
Edgeborough School, Farnham

Zookeeper

Z ookeepers are the best
O ver the hills
O ver the hills are zebras
K eeper feeding
E njoy the zoo
E njoy seeing the animals
P enguins, you can see
E lephants are playing
R unning zebras on the field.

Tilly Vincent (6)
Edgeborough School, Farnham

New Zealand

N ew day is waiting
E nd of the day
W hen planes come

Z ipping along
E nd of the journey
A nd sweet air
L ong airport
A long the road
N ow you are waiting
D ay is done.

Hugo Steele (6)
Edgeborough School, Farnham

Friends

F unny friends
R unning and playing
I t's fun to have a friend
E very one is a great friend
N ever biting people
D o not say unkind words to your teacher
S o many people are friends.

Max Kimberley-Bowen (6)
Edgeborough School, Farnham

Football

F ancy goal
O ur team is Man City
O ur team is going to win
T he other team won
B eautiful trophy
A ll for them
L ucky them
L ovely team.

Reyan Patel (7)
Edgeborough School, Farnham

Trucks

T remendous trucks are strong
R umbling along the road
U p and down every day
C rushing up boulders
K eeping its loads in
S eeing everyone as he drives past.

Hugo Peachey (6)
Edgeborough School, Farnham

Leopard

L eopards are very cute
E legant, brave and cool
O n our Planet Earth
P erfectly fiesty
A nd very deadly
R acing around the plains
D roughts.

Lachlan Mackenzie (6)
Edgeborough School, Farnham

Brother

B rother is cool
R eally good at games
O lder than me
T all!
H e is twenty
E ating pasta together
R eally makes me happy.

Jeremy Kelly (6)
Edgeborough School, Farnham

Ukraine

U nder the sky
K illing the Ukrainians
R ifles shooting
A nd bombing
I n the moonlight
N o hope
E nd the war!

Percy Sadler (6)
Edgeborough School, Farnham

Castles

C astles
A moat
S ome turrets
T owering high
L ong staircases
E nd of the battle
S ome archers.

Hamish Hudson (6)
Edgeborough School, Farnham

Fairies

F ast
A mazing
I nvisible
R eal
I ncredible magic
E very day, the fairy flies
S ilver wings.

Emmie Gottschalk (6)
Edgeborough School, Farnham

Tigers

T ough
I n the zoo
G rowling to flee
E ndangered animals
R escuers helping them
S cary as a python.

Liam Siegele (7)
Edgeborough School, Farnham

Bear

B ig bears are humungous
E verywhere is loud with bears
A ggressive stomping
R eally big feet.

Hugo Dewé-Roux (6)
Edgeborough School, Farnham

Star

S hiny beautiful stars
T he stars are in the sky
A mazing stars
R ound the sun, they fly.

Rita Carlile (6)
Edgeborough School, Farnham

Army

A mazing machine guns
R ifles shooting
M y walkie-talkie
Y oung men fighting.

Laurence Fisher (7)
Edgeborough School, Farnham

Mermaid

M agic flows beneath the deep blue sea
E meralds lie on the ocean floor
R attling rocks beneath the ocean
M ermaids under the deep blue sea
A n oyster under the deep blue sea, a pearl lying inside
I n the ocean, there was a mermaid palace
D id you see one?

Lyla-Mae Reynolds (6)
Hebburn Lakes Primary School, Hebburn

Rainbow Friends

R unning fast
A mazing
I ndependent
N ice
B rilliant
O ctopus
W illing to share

F riends
R ainbow colours
I ncredible
E xcellent
N ames
D oing their best
S ave it.

Miller McGonnell (6)
Hebburn Lakes Primary School, Hebburn

Zookeeper

Z oos are great!
O rangutans are cheeky
O tters run wild
K eep the animals safe and fed
E veryone helps to care for the animals
E lephants are my favourite
P eople come to visit
E veryone is kind
R eally good fun!

Alisha Marshall (6)
Hebburn Lakes Primary School, Hebburn

Autumn

A utumn leaves are orange
U p above, the conkers sit waiting
T rees as beautiful as they can be
U p above you is a beautiful sky
M y little face is as beautiful as the sky
N ow in a mirror, you look as beautiful as can be.

Hannah Davison (6)
Hebburn Lakes Primary School, Hebburn

Pandas

P andas are my favourite animal
A nd they like to climb
N ot the smartest animal
D efinitely cute
A funny creature
S ometimes eat pumpkins.

Luke Craig (6)
Hebburn Lakes Primary School, Hebburn

Dancing

D ance is fun
A new dance routine
N ever give up
C onfidence is key
I nclude my friends
N ice tutus
G reat times, I've had.

Jessica Casey (6)
Hebburn Lakes Primary School, Hebburn

Gymnast

G reat fun
Y oung or old
M any coloured leotards
N ice and relaxing
A mazing
S trong skills
T eaching instructors.

Millie-Rae Halliday (6)
Hebburn Lakes Primary School, Hebburn

Dance

D ance is my favourite
A lways grooving
N ever stop moving
C razy shapes and fun music
E very day, we learn new moves.

Faye Whitehead (6)
Hebburn Lakes Primary School, Hebburn

Bluey

B luey makes me happy
L ovely and kind
U nderstanding and a good listener
E veryone loves her
Y ou make me laugh.

Sophie Crumbie (6)
Hebburn Lakes Primary School, Hebburn

Fast

F irst place is where I want to be
A mazing all who see me
S uper speed is how I roll
T aking over everyone in my path.

Erica Robertson (6)
Hebburn Lakes Primary School, Hebburn

Space

S pace is awesome
P lanets have aliens
A stronauts go in rockets
C an I catch a star?
E arth is our planet.

Kendall Smurthwaite (6)
Hebburn Lakes Primary School, Hebburn

Hopper

H ops
O utside
P laying
P aper chase
E veryone
R uns.

Phoebe Lumley (6)
Hebburn Lakes Primary School, Hebburn

Messi

M y favourite player
E nergy
S kill
S cores goals
I nspires me.

Kade Loughran (6)
Hebburn Lakes Primary School, Hebburn

Chocolate

C hocolate is yummy and melty
H aving chocolate ice cream for dinner is my dream!
O range is a flavour that tastes trash
C hildren with chocolate all over their faces
O pening wrappers is noisy
L icking delicious chocolate!
A milkshake is my favourite style
T here is a chocolate city
E veryone loves chocolate!

Sienna Connelly (7)
Kirn Primary School, Kirn

Ice Lolly

I ce lollies are sticky!
C hildren eating in the sun
E very drip tastes so good

L ovely bubblegum is delicious
O range is good
L emon is a flavour I detest!
L icking and licking until it's done
Y ummy any time of the day.

Ella Dickson (6)
Kirn Primary School, Kirn

Wrestler

W restling is fake
R hea is the best on the roster
E veryone eliminates their opponent
S pecial people win the Royal Rumble
T ears are shed when they lose
L osers get booed!
E ach winner celebrates
R eady to take on the next.

Rory Gray (7)
Kirn Primary School, Kirn

Banana

B ananas are healthy
A nd they are cool
N ever let a banana dance!
A green banana should never be eaten
N ice and yellow, tastes so sweet
A nd can make a tasty treat.

Jay Mackay (6)
Kirn Primary School, Kirn

Dragon

D ragons are faster than sound
R unning after dragon trappers
A lways breathing lightning
G reat big wings
O nly eats fish
N obody dares to touch her.

Dylan Stevenson (7)
Kirn Primary School, Kirn

Greece

G oing to Greece
R eally sunny and warm
E very day, I will swim
E ven at night-time
C hocolate ice cream every day
E vening strolls along the beach.

Suri McGinnigal (6)
Kirn Primary School, Kirn

Spider

S piders are scary!
P eering through their tiny eyes
I run away when they come near!
D oing scary stuff
E very leg is hairy
R eally, really scary!

Alyvia Larkins (7)
Kirn Primary School, Kirn

Kind

K indness is caring for everyone!
I love helping my mummy
N ever be perfect
D on't just dream about being kind, do something kind every day!

Bjorn Collier (6)
Kirn Primary School, Kirn

Monster

M onster jam
O h no!
N oisy engines
S and is there
T hey are scary
E veryone screams
R eally cool backflips!

Mason MacLean (6)
Kirn Primary School, Kirn

Disney

D ream of Disney
I would like to go
S ome princesses and sprinkles
N ew characters
E xciting big castle
Y ou can play!

Sara Brivkalns (6)
Kirn Primary School, Kirn

Slime

S lime is slimy and sticky
L ots of colours
I t is stretchy
M y favourite is purple and glittery
E ven play with it at bedtime.

Ella Campbell (6)
Kirn Primary School, Kirn

Stitch

S titch is fluffy
T wo big ears
I s blue and pink
T wo big eyes
C ute
H e makes me happy.

Emily Kennedy (7)
Kirn Primary School, Kirn

Toys

T oys are playful
O wn teddies and play at night
Y ou can build stuff
S oldiers shoot each other in games.

Fergus Allison (7)
Kirn Primary School, Kirn

Army

A lot of soldiers
R eady to fight
M any men are hiding
Y ou will never find them.

Andrew Gorman (6)
Kirn Primary School, Kirn

Lava

L ava is long
A hot glue nobody can touch
V olcanoes explode
A lways burning.

Arlo Poynter-Dalton (7)
Kirn Primary School, Kirn

Superpower

S uper reader
U nbelievable at the splits
P rincess of kittens
E veryone is friendly to me
R eally like Daddy and Mummy to hug me
P olite and loves to play
O h and I really like Lottie
W illing to win trophies and medals
E very day, I talk to people
R eally... I don't like tidying.

Felicia Wang (6)
Portsmouth High School, Southsea

Superpower

S uper Peony loves her friends
U m, do you like my dress?
P retty
E xcellent at gymnastics
R eally good at riding my bike
P opular
O h yeah, I can do cartwheels
W heeee! I love swinging on the swing so high
E xcellent at drawing
R eady to learn.

Peony Marsh (5)
Portsmouth High School, Southsea

Superpower

S ofia is super at sports
U nbelievable at cartwheels
P erfect at swimming
E xcellent at tennis
R eally good at hockey
P retending to be a spy
O ften hungry
W inning at sports
E ntering competitions
R eally sleepy sometimes.

Sofia Kadinopoulos (5)
Portsmouth High School, Southsea

Superpower

S uper-duper
U sually really good at reading
P olite
E veryone's friend
R eading superstar
P erfect friend
O ften with my mummy
W ild with words
E njoy playing with my brother and sister
R eally like to try new foods.

Addison Knight (6)
Portsmouth High School, Southsea

Superpower

S oftly, my toes balance
U nbelievably good listener
P robably taking risks
E nergetic
R uns bats and ball races
P ainting Payton
O utside in the playground
W hizzing slowly everywhere
E veryone is kind
R oaring around.

Payton Law (6)
Portsmouth High School, Southsea

Superpower

S uper at swimming underwater
U nicorn loving
P opping bubbles in the rain
E xcellent at gymnastics
R unning fast
P retty hair
O ften kind
W ent on the trampoline
E very day, I do exercise
R eally good at running.

Lula Peck (5)
Portsmouth High School, Southsea

Superpower

S uper at headstands
U nbelievable
P erfect
E very day, I am kind
R unning fast
P retty purple and pink
O utside doing the monkey bars
W ith my family at the park
E nd of the day
R eally kind and caring.

Blossom Morgan (5)
Portsmouth High School, Southsea

Superpower

S uper speedy swimmer
U p in the air saving the day
P icture diary
E very day, I am saving
R ock climber
P arent power
O h, power time
W ow, super days
E xcellent swinging
R ock star on my guitar.

Alazne Currie (5)
Portsmouth High School, Southsea

Superpower

S uper speed
U p in the air in a hot-air balloon
P olite
E xcellent climbing power
R eally nice power
P erfect power
O ften kind
W iggle and jiggle
E xcellent scooter riding
R ock it out power.

Olivia Cullen-Taylor (6)
Portsmouth High School, Southsea

Superpower

S uper swimming
U p in the sky
P eaceful reader
E xcellent at climbing
R eading books in the library
P laying Frozen
O ften helping people
W hizzing around
E xcited
R olling on the trampoline.

Mateya Asenov (5)
Portsmouth High School, Southsea

Superpower

S uper singer
U nderstands others' feelings
P ositive
E xcited about finishing my book
R eally good at being a friend
P olite
O rganised
W illing to please
E njoy cookery
R eady to learn.

Betty Woolridge (6)
Portsmouth High School, Southsea

Superpower

S uperheroes
U nderwater in the swimming pool
P op the bubbles
E xcellent play
R eally kind to my friends
P roud
O ff flying
W hen I help people
E ven when I see my friends
R eally special.

Ava Norris (5)
Portsmouth High School, Southsea

Superpower

S uper speed
U nbelievably kind
P erfect life-saving
E very day, I save the day
R unning
P erfect at listening
O ften running
W ith my friends, I play
E xcellent at learning
R eally good.

Neve Worrall (5)
Portsmouth High School, Southsea

Superpower

S uper swimmer
U pside down on the bars
P owers are great
E very person has one
R eady for reading
P retty princess
O rganised
W arrior
E verybody is great
R eally ready for everything.

Abbiah Gunton (7)
Portsmouth High School, Southsea

Superpower

S uper-duper me
U nderstanding things
P retty drawings
E veryone makes friends
R eally fast at running
P ainting power
O riginal me
W ander around things
E veryone talks
R acing power.

Ruona Osigho (6)
Portsmouth High School, Southsea

Superpower

S uper singer
U nbelievable maths
P ainting
E veryone's friends
R acing my dad
P olite
O livia is always my friend
W ishing on some stars
E njoy cookery
R eally good at Lego.

Hallie Lewis-Gregory (7)
Portsmouth High School, Southsea

Superpower

S peedy footballer
U nbelievably good listener
P erfectly kind
E specially fast
R unning fast
P ushing hard
O ver and over
W inning trophies
E xhausted and tired
R eading books.

Layla Belcher (6)
Portsmouth High School, Southsea

Superpower

S eriously silly
U nbelievable at baking
P erfect pal
E nergetic
R aphaella
P uppy lover
O nesie wearer
W onderful
E xciting entertainer
R aphaella the rule breaker.

Raphaella Tozzi (7)
Portsmouth High School, Southsea

Superpower

S wimming speedily
U nderwater
P owerful arms
E pic!
R ound, round
P uffing harder
O nly to jump into
W ater waving
E verywhere Alba Angelic
R oaring with laughter.

Alba Shireby (6)
Portsmouth High School, Southsea

Alton Towers

A lton Towers has rides
L ots of fun
T erribly scary rides
O nly go down if you are brave
N emesis was Mummy's favourite

T ons of people go every year
O blivion is really fast
W e always have so much fun
E xtraordinary rides
R unaway Mine Train is my favourite
S miler is a crazy ride.

Edward Crawford (6)
St Joseph's Catholic Primary School, Uttoxeter

Crocodiles

C rocodiles are scary
R eally sharp teeth
O liver's running away now!
C limbing up a tree
O h my gosh, he's coming!
D on't look down
I am scared
L eaves are falling down
E ek! The branch is breaking!
S *plash!* Swim, swim away.

Oliver Rathbone (6)
St Joseph's Catholic Primary School, Uttoxeter

Roller Coaster

R eally fast
O ut of this world
L ots of fun
L oop the loops
E xciting
R apid motion

C urves and bends
O ptimum fun
A dventurous
S uper steep drops
T errifying
E verlasting queues
R ides rule!

Arthur McNicol (6)
St Joseph's Catholic Primary School, Uttoxeter

Australia

A ustralia is hot
U nder the trees, koalas live
S unny days
T he sharks swim the seas
R angers look out for kangaroos
A turtle and clownfish in the sea
L ots of koalas have been rescued
I n and out of the waves
A wildfire in the bush.

Bodhi Raby (6)
St Joseph's Catholic Primary School, Uttoxeter

Disneyland

D ream to visit
I mportant day
S urprise for me
N ew impression
E xciting moment
Y ou're on an unforgettable trip
L ovely choice
A ttractions are very interesting
N ever-ending fun
D esire is there will be a result.

Katya Pastushenko (8)
St Joseph's Catholic Primary School, Uttoxeter

Birthdays

B irthdays are the best
I let my friends come
R unning around
T hen we have some cake
H appy birthday to me
D o lots of games
A nd pass the parcel
Y ou can have a party bag
S ee what gifts I have.

Arla Fearnett (6)
St Joseph's Catholic Primary School, Uttoxeter

Crocodile

C roc in the swamp
R un for your life
O h my gosh
C roc in the swamp
O h my gosh
D o not dive into the swamp
I f you get too close, they will snap
L ong, scaly tails
E ek! Run for your life!

Freddie Sutton (6)
St Joseph's Catholic Primary School, Uttoxeter

Designer

D esigners are really cool
E ven design diggers
S omeday, I want to be one
I will need to learn lots
G et good at making things
N eed to manage projects
E ven test the machines
R eally like this job.

Ginny Rushton (6)
St Joseph's Catholic Primary School, Uttoxeter

Liverpool

L ike a star
I mpossible victories
V ery, very fast Mo Salah
E uropean champions
R ed for home
P remier League champions
O ur club
O n Stanley Park
L uis Díaz scoring goals.

Evie Gill (6)
St Joseph's Catholic Primary School, Uttoxeter

Frozen

F rozen icicles all around the theatre
R eally excited children sitting in their seats
O laf, Sven and Kristoff singing songs
Z ap the magic and snow falls
E lsa and Anna are sisters forever
N ow, let it go.

Ella Peach (6)
St Joseph's Catholic Primary School, Uttoxeter

Alton Towers

A mazing rides
L augher
T ime-consuming
O verjoyed
N imble rides

T errific
O utstanding experience
W onderful
E xcitement
R avishing
S uper.

Jozef Korista-Redfern (6)
St Joseph's Catholic Primary School, Uttoxeter

Dinosaurs

D inosaurs eat each other
I like dinosaurs
N ot scared of them
O nly in the dark
S uper strong
A rghhhh!
U nder the hot sun
R *oar!*
S upersaurus!

Louis Matthew Young (6)
St Joseph's Catholic Primary School, Uttoxeter

Gymnast

G etting ready in my leotard
Y o-yoing around the bar
M aking moves on the beam
N ot a minute to waste
A mess with all the chalk
S tretching out my splits
T rophy time.

Ashleigh Roberts (6)
St Joseph's Catholic Primary School, Uttoxeter

Unicorns

U nusual creature
N ever seen
I love them
C aps, they can't wear
O ften in dreams
R ainbow hair
N ever go
S afe with me.

Cora McCutcheon (6)
St Joseph's Catholic Primary School, Uttoxeter

Dancer

D reaming about dance
A ll day long
N eat arms and pointy toes
C ostumes, hair and make-up
E verything ready
R ound and round, I twirl and whirl!

Phoebe Grattage (6)
St Joseph's Catholic Primary School, Uttoxeter

Actress

A ctresses tell a story
C reative dancing
T alented storytellers
R eally amazing
E xtremely good
S uper singers
S pecial performance.

Iona O'Neill (6)
St Joseph's Catholic Primary School, Uttoxeter

Singer

S inging makes me feel good
I love singing
N ever stop singing
G oing to be a singer
E very day, I sing
R emember, singing makes you happy.

Irina Babacea (6)
St Joseph's Catholic Primary School, Uttoxeter

Police

P eople call me for help
O ur police car is fast
L ooking out for robbers
I have handcuffs
C all me on 999
E veryone can hear my sirens.

Beau Bromage (6)
St Joseph's Catholic Primary School, Uttoxeter

Holiday

H appiness
O cean
L azy days
I love planes
D ays at the beach
A lways by the pool
Y ummy ice cream.

Freddie H (6)
St Joseph's Catholic Primary School, Uttoxeter

Cats

C ats are lovely
A t Kitty Cafe, I meet cats
T hey are sweet and fluffy
S ometimes they are predatory.

Freya Jeziorska (6)
St Joseph's Catholic Primary School, Uttoxeter

Vet

V ipers are wriggly for vets
E lephants are looked at using a ladder
T igers like showing me their sharp teeth.

Perrie Stephens (6)
St Joseph's Catholic Primary School, Uttoxeter

Ronaldo

R eader
O f
N otable
A crostic
L et's
D o it
O kay.

Shayne Felix Fernandes (6)
St Joseph's Catholic Primary School, Uttoxeter

Superhero

S liding into bed
U sually, I save people
P eople are the ones I help
E very person, I love
R eading, I let people read
H urt, I stop people getting hurt
E veryone is safe
R eally help people
O h, I help people that are my fans.

Hannah Bushby (6)
St Patrick's RC Primary School, Consett

Unicorn

U sually sparkling bright at night
N ight-time, it comes out to play
I t goes back in the early morning
C utely, it sits next to me
O h no, it's morning again!
R eally worried about my unicorn
N ever came back again.

Evie Henderson (7)
St Patrick's RC Primary School, Consett

Footballer

F ootballer
O ff the keeper
O ver the keeper
T op corner
B all
A ttacker
L eft wing
L eft back
E xtra time
R ight back.

Harry Richardson (6)
St Patrick's RC Primary School, Consett

Disneyland

D reamland
I sabel
S titch
N emo
E xcited
Y our favourite things
L ilo
A dventureland
N ew stuff
D elicious food.

Lydia Murphy (6)
St Patrick's RC Primary School, Consett

Cybertruck

C yber
Y ou will like them
B ig truck
E xtremely scary
R eally big
T ruck
R acing
U nbelievable
C ar
K ing car.

James Ellison (6)
St Patrick's RC Primary School, Consett

Princess

P retty and respectful
R oyalty
I ndividual
N ecklace
C inderella
E xtremely posh
S o kind, helpful and caring
S parkly shoes.

Amelia Tennant (6)
St Patrick's RC Primary School, Consett

Treats

T o help the world
R eady to save animals
E very day, I am going to help
A vet helps animals
T o save animals
S ave animals.

Daisy Cooke (6)
St Patrick's RC Primary School, Consett

Heights

H arsh injury
E veryone could get hurt
I ncredibly scary
G rowing buildings
H elp people in danger
T all
S cary.

Kaylam-James Walton (7)
St Patrick's RC Primary School, Consett

Excited

E xtreme sports
X -ray
C aterpillar
I ce cream
T o go to the movies
E xtremely fun
D oing stuff with my friend.

Rhys Hughes (6)
St Patrick's RC Primary School, Consett

Princess

P alace
R oyal
I n a castle
N ecklace
C astle
E xtremely happy
S o helpful
S parkly nice shoes.

Ivy Dorritt (6)
St Patrick's RC Primary School, Consett

Football

F ree-kick
O ffside
O ver the time
T eam
B all
A ttacker
L ights
L inesman.

Jamie Dixon (6)
St Patrick's RC Primary School, Consett

Ronaldo

R onaldo
O utside the box
N ice tap-ins
A mazing
L a Liga
D efender
O pening doors.

Theo Spencer (6)
St Patrick's RC Primary School, Consett

Princess

P alace
R eally nice
I sla
N oble
C rown
E legant
S pecial
S mart.

Tia-Louise Hester (6)
St Patrick's RC Primary School, Consett

Flying

F airy
L ight night
Y ellow wings
I ncredibly exciting
N ew shiny teeth
G ust of wind.

Aria Joyce (6)
St Patrick's RC Primary School, Consett

Dragons

D arkness
R oars
A mazing
G reen spikes
O h no, help me!
N ot nice
S cary.

Noah Edward (6)
St Patrick's RC Primary School, Consett

Cars

C ars beep
A larm rings very loudly
R acing cars
S ome people scream in cars.

Oliver O'Keefe (7)
St Patrick's RC Primary School, Consett

Match

M bappé
A ttacker
T op corner
C entre forward
H igh score.

Joseph Richardson (6)
St Patrick's RC Primary School, Consett

Slime

S ticky
L ong
I love it
M ushy
E very day, it's a rainbow.

George Wilson (6)
St Patrick's RC Primary School, Consett

Stars

S parkly
T errific
A mazing
R ush through the sky
S hining.

Isla-Grace Robinson (6)
St Patrick's RC Primary School, Consett

Ghost

G hostly
H ouse
O h, I'm scared
S cary
T errifying.

Lydia O'Rourke (6)
St Patrick's RC Primary School, Consett

Dog

D oor
O utside
G rowl.

Ella MacGregor (7)
St Patrick's RC Primary School, Consett

Danger Zone

D istant missiles
A ircraft taking off
N avigation lights in the night
G iant explosions on the ground
E nergetic engines
R oaring like tigers

Z ooming through the air
O ver enemy targets
N oisy planes everywhere
E ngage in another dogfight.

Odysseas Papamichos Chronakis (6)
Staines Preparatory School, Knowle Green

Footballer

F riends made
O n the pitch
O utdoors or indoors
T rain together
B e top of the league
A mazing goals
L ike Cristiano Ronaldo
L oves the sport
E xtra time is exciting
R eferee rules the game!

Rohan Sharma (6)
Staines Preparatory School, Knowle Green

Christmas

C hristmas carols
H olly on the door
R eading stories
I am wrapping presents
S nowflakes falling down
T ime for hot chocolate
M erry Christmas everyone
A dorable reindeer
S anta comes soon.

Maitreyi Patil (6)
Staines Preparatory School, Knowle Green

Love

L ove comes from hearts, love does not split into parts
O ur superpower is love, that's God's message from above
V elvety, velvety, gives us security
"**E** veryone deserves some pure love," says God from above.

Zoie Pitroda (6)
Staines Preparatory School, Knowle Green

Holiday

H olidays are fun
O n the hot beach
L icking ice lollies every day
I *love* it
D ancing in the evening
A nd having late dinners
Y ippee! I am going on holiday soon!

Bella Patel (6)
Staines Preparatory School, Knowle Green

Wimbledon

W inner
I n the final
M atch
B rings back a
L arge
E legant
D azzling trophy
O nce he is declared the champion
N irbhay Singh!

Nirbhay Singh (6)
Staines Preparatory School, Knowle Green

Family

F un times together
A lways love being together
M ummy's warm huggles in bed
I n the park playing
L aughing and playing
Y ay, a yummy feast with my family!

Leya Kareer Gupta (6)
Staines Preparatory School, Knowle Green

Flying

F ly up high
L ook at me in the sky
Y ou can see the clouds below
I can feel the cold wind blow
N ow I'm like a bird, so free
G oing fast, look at me!

Arjan Gill (6)
Staines Preparatory School, Knowle Green

Scary

S carecrows in the field
C hildren are afraid
A nimals are hiding
R ain pouring down
Y ou must stay away!

Tawanda Tapiwa (6)
Staines Preparatory School, Knowle Green

Young Writers Information

We hope you have enjoyed reading this book – and that you will continue to in the coming years.

If you're the parent or family member of an enthusiastic poet or story writer, do visit our website **www.youngwriters.co.uk/subscribe** and sign up to receive news, competitions, writing challenges and tips, activities and much, much more! There's lots to keep budding writers motivated!

If you would like to order further copies of this book, or any of our other titles, then please give us a call or order via your online account.

Young Writers
Remus House
Coltsfoot Drive
Peterborough
PE2 9BF
(01733) 890066
info@youngwriters.co.uk

Join in the conversation!
Tips, news, giveaways and much more!

YoungWritersUK   YoungWritersCW   youngwriterscw
youngwriterscw   youngwriterscw-uk